Cupid's Arrow

Poems of Love

First published 2020 by The Hedgehog Poetry Press

Published in the UK by
The Hedgehog Poetry Press
5, Coppack House
Churchill Avenue
Clevedon
BS21 6QW

www.hedgehogpress.co.uk

ISBN: 978-1-913499-56-3

A CIP Catalogue record for this book is available from the British
Library.

Contents:

OZ HARDWICK

Love In The Digital Season

To everything a season. Poetry is dead on the vine, so now it's time to count blessings. My grandmother was better at this than me, counting them like sheep nimbly jumping a picket fence until she fell asleep for ever, but I can't remember anything from her list, even though she told me time and time again. So I start with breathing and having enough food, and then the short walk to the park which is reborn every two or three days. At this point I'm not sure whether I'm awake or dreaming, so I add this comforting uncertainty to the list, just after the shelves full of books and music. Though I've always run with scissors, most of the scars have healed, so that must count for something; then there's the way I hear voices in car engines and condemned buildings. The voices in my head are a mixed blessing, but a blessing nonetheless, and if I was writing these down, I would dip my pen in blue ink and turn to a fresh page before making notes on the way that your voice is out of sync with your lips when you laugh and dismiss each small act of beauty. This is where I lose count, so I open the gate and let sheep wander where they will. It's unseasonably cold, and I watch as your Zoom-frozen face breaks into hundreds – maybe thousands – of bright patches.

EILEEN CARNEY HULME

Choosing a Stone

What would you say to me
now, that I looked too closely
at the moon and when my heart
quickened did you bend
to kiss me, unfolding stars
that leapt from the sky
during a cloudburst,
their fate undecided.

Listen, nothing matters
the breeze through
marram grass carries our love
and in the sometime
that was never our time
you will still skim stones
and turn to me
with your half smile.

POPPY-JAYNE JONES

Rockhollow Series: Husbandry

My husband is an oak tree.
He has been an oak tree as long as I've known him,
when I was a split tendril pulling away from a tribe,
when I was painted in weed-killer one Summer.

He was an oak I watched,
deep within a thicket of unprofitable trees, ivy suckers trembling.
I crept, wrapped my heart-shaped thighs about him and free-climbed,
thriving, squeezing his body with my body.

I'm morose by nature,
have a tendency to suffocate dreams
while he sleeps and I grow loose curls
staring through a leafy headboard, watching falling stars.

My husband is wild of the well rooted kind,
hundred years of family history behind him,
hundred years of strong seasons ahead,
unknowingly starved of sunshine.

I'd be lesser without him
ramble along the dirt, thirsty and languid,
hunting for a less tolerable fit.
I wonder if I'd even find it.

My husband is often unaware
of the eco system he supports,
roots connecting canals, shade roofing houses
and so I nurture an oak tree. I feel obligated.

In a few years I'll bury it beyond the garden gate
creating a version of us, or at least him,
to root down and watch over the land we shared
years after worms have made liquid gold of us both.

VIC PICKUP

Him, building me a bookcase

Sixteen chunky shelves, propped on blocks
of pallet wood, sliced like angel cakes –
each one a different shade.

A dusty finger pins the glossy pages
of a how-to book. Cautiously, he drills,
but soon his eye is fixed, unblinking.

The bar turns, the wood secured in its vice.
Lines of sinew flicker in his forearm as he saws,
then blows and smooths the debris clear.

He measures with one eye shut,
improvises in places where
the spirit level would not go.

He gives purpose to timber fit only for the fire,
a hand-me-down drill and screws
from an ice cream tub on a garage shelf.

Having masked the edges, he applies three coats,
wearing war paint of magnolia, the glean of cream
laden thickly on his brush.

We stand and my hand slides
into his back pocket, already wondering
which will go where and in what order.

He doesn't know, but this is my greatest wish:
not the having of a place
or a way to keep things, only this –

Him, building me a bookcase.

PATRICIA M OSBORNE

All I have to do is Dream

My stomach ferments
as you chat to glamorous girls.

'We're finished,' I say, slinging
my handbag at your head.

You agree it's time to split
leaving me in pieces.

All I have to do is dream
spins on the record player.

No more sipping cider, curling
up together on the couch.

No more hugs and kisses
in the back row of the Pictures.

No one to cuddle to keep me warm
walking in the snow and rain.

Teenagers dance in pairs
at the church youth club

but I stand alone
handbag close to my chest.

ANTHONY PATICCHIO

We Are Riding the Paris Pike, May 24, 1987

We are riding the Paris Pike
back to Lexington
trailing a cast tin bucket,
unaware of the racket
sparking in our wake.

Left behind,

the morning's first roses cut
in Nell Collins' garden,
the gathered daughters,
their daughters and sons,
the noonday shower
settling in the heat,

all that brought us here
this late May afternoon.

Your still
deciding smile
wakens me now.

All manner of things changed,
though not this day.

We are standing together,
curious,
holding hands,
listening.

In a near hallway
Kitty is singing quietly
to Nell –

"My Old Kentucky Home"—

It is no more than a whisper
at the center of all the day's deciding.

Later, on the highway,
drawing an ancient bucket
toward our lives together,

I hear only the
whisper of our promise.

Sparks fly
from the pavement,
surround us,

we are on our way.

GAYNOR KANE

Bridge:

> a construction spanning a divide, supporting the ends;
> an arch;
> a connection

for Michael

Twenty-one years ago
we stood on the edge
of Devil's Bridge, on the edge
of the Atlantic, at the edge
of Antigua with nothing
between there and Europe
except enormity of marriage and sea.

The rocks, the vast ocean,
in iron grey, dark blue and violet tones of iolite.
Water sapphire, gemstone which symbolises
our time together,
the *Viking's compass*,
they first used slivers as polarising filters
to navigate the seas.

We stood, still, hand in hand.
listening to crashing waves
on the underside of the arch;
watching water whistle through blowholes,
we felt salt on our skin.

Hand in hand, we'd made a pact,
we knew we were jumping
off the edge together, into a life where
everything would be alright if we just held
each other, if we just held
each other's hand.

There will be time,
there will be time for more,
there will be time for more trips to the edge,
time for more bridges,
for more pacts.

RACHAEL CHARLOTTE

Tacenda

Too much make-up, black leather,
disco smoke January mist; in your eyes
the same violent animal, suffering
in the vacant blackness.
This is the closest thing isn't it?

The horsehair vest of your gaze;
how bold to imagine your bare chest –
thick, black hair, a gold chain hanging
around your neck, your un-socked feet
on the bathroom floor, to not retreat, to stand tall

in silence. Loud denial caught coughing,
something psychoanalysts talk about
is in the world now.
I am coughing
and coughing to stop you hearing:

the palm of my hand against your cheek,
my forehead pressed lightly to yours,
the hot dampness of my breath on your lips,
my fingers sliding underneath your shirt,
the entire weight of my head on your shoulder.

Tell me stories from your childhood
& about the times you have cried,
tell me what you would do if...
I want to be your favourite songs & your favourite books
& for people to look

at us & think, *aren't they pretty?*
For them not to know what we really are,
how much harder it makes
everything, I ask too much, I know I do but
to touch you – just once...

MARGARET ROYALL

A Box of Precious Secrets

Inside a drawer in grandma's house I found
A secret box with tokens from a tryst
On thinning parchment, delicately bound

Victorian love chains, beautifully wound
A lock of hair that he had often kissed
Inside a drawer in grandma's house I found

My heart stood still, I dared not make a sound
Exploring these fond memories of bliss
On thinning parchment, delicately bound

A photo of her kneeling on the ground
Hair flowing free in strands of golden mist
Inside a drawer in grandma's house I found

Two hearts in decoupage on Cupid's mound
With spidery writing, hard to catch the gist
On thinning parchment delicately bound

I sensed that love was dancing all around
Enchanted by this unexpected gift
Inside a drawer in grandma's house I found
On thinning parchment delicately bound

CEINWEN E CARIAD HAYDON

Love Reimagined

Her lovers' faces shift form, hide, and seek
her all her life's long days. She is possessed
by hauntings. Longings stir, make her limbs weak –
memories outpaced by paths unprogressed.

In old age, their names meld: her mind repaints
incidents and places, conceives strange scenes.
Kaleidoscope-love dances unrestrained,
surreal configurations flood dreams.

Has she but one love, reincarnated ...
or did polyamory call her name.
Monogamy's ties left her frustrated
yet her husband's fingers always remain

shadowed on her gentle-stroked hair and skin.
Him. Last, best. Her true one. Without, within.

JULIE ANNE GILLIGAN

FOUR-OH-FOUR ERROR: A Song to my Search Engine

'Unrequited love is the infinite curse of a lonely heart' Christina Westover

You are my one and only, my sole search engine, you alone
haul the train of my thoughts through the arachnid-netted universe.
We became coupled, I unwittingly. You used cookies to entice me
into places that would never otherwise appear on my menu.

You geotargeted my inbound link with accuracy; you tempt me
beyond social media; we are in tandem in our empathy of algorhythms.
You are my pioneer, going before me, testing my privacy settings.
What meta tags I have are yours: you have all my title tags.

Tracks are everywhere, some set to mislead; many pages never found,
but you are my surfboard, my anchor text. My keyword is you:
my ways are optimised. Sadly I am but one in a million players
on your multiplatform four-dimensional gameboard. You toy with me.

I am merely a mouse in the maw of infinity
always in search of the Engineer.

C.B SEARLE

aim high

aim high
she said

but you
are the sun
the moon
and the stars
I said

aim high
she said

ROMINA VAN MAAREN

Time travelling

Californian dreams
of butterfly music
She sings in the shower
of colours in skies
against the memories
as ribbons of clouds

Some people love the sand
and some live in it only
a riverride away from the
Angels' tears Yet once
you've dipped your toe
in the pool you are lost
Winter waves still sweet
She loves to settle the red
with a pink In the shade
While the elegant fragrance
through the open windows

The rain check became
a sun check with him
This life of her mind
His love in her life